ADVANCE PRAISE FOR DAILY MIRACLES

"The opportunity to care for people is a sacred trust and a privilege that allows us to grow spiritually and professionally. These authors have captured those moments and distilled from them a beautiful philosophy to guide our practice to a higher level."

– Karlene M. Kerfoot, PhD, RN, CNAA, FAAN
Principal, Kerfoot & Associates, Inc.

"Daily Miracles is a gift celebrating the soul of nursing. In an era where business demands, technological interventions, and limited time and resources define the patient-care environment, these wonderful stories and inspirational pictures reflect the beautiful 'inner landscape' that resides within the heart of every nurse. It reveals the intent and the compassion of those who offer a healing presence to the world."

– JoEllen Koerner, PhD, RN, FAAN
President and Chief Executive Officer, Nurse MetriX

"Daily Miracles is more than a miracle. It is a glowing product of vision, perseverance, courage, devotion, and art."

– Linda Hawes Clever, MD
President, RENEW

D0109562

"I received Daily Miracles and read it through several times, marveling at the stories and the beautiful accompanying photographs. Today, I took the book to work to show my staff the untapped power that lies within each of them. THANK YOU FOR THE PERFECT GIFT!"

— Polly Gates, RN, MPA/HSA, FACHE
Regional Patient Care Services Workforce Director, Kaiser Permanente

"Daily Miracles tells a story that is seldom, if ever, told. The human experience of compassion and caring is lived with no greater intensity than in the relationship between nurse and patient. In the retelling of events of caring, the capacity for one human being to unconditionally serve another becomes bigger than life. Every nurse deserves to find her- or himself in this amazing book. Every nurse lives in the stunning tales and images and can be celebrated in ways not often enough shared. It captures the authenticity of nursing that Florence Nightingale envisioned and that each nurse offers each day in hospitals around the world."

— Susan E. Mazer, MA
President and Chief Executive Officer
Healing HealthCare Systems
http://www.healinghealth.com

DAILY MIRACLES

Stories and Practices of Humanity and Excellence in Health Care

Alan Briskin, PhD and Jan Boller, RN, PhD

Sigma Theta Tau International
Honor Society of Nursing®

DEDICATION

The Universe is made of stories, not of atoms.

– Muriel Rukeyser

We dedicate this book to the storytellers and to the stories that make up our world,
providing us hope, making us laugh, and reminding us of our common humanity,
in sickness and in health. May these stories travel with us,
spark our hearts, and help us notice daily miracles.

SIGMA THETA TAU INTERNATIONAL

Editor-in-Chief: Jeff Burnham
Acquisitions Editor: Fay L. Bower, DNSc, FAAN
Project Editor: Carla Hall
Proofreader: Jane Palmer

Project concept, collaboration, and design by Silverleaf Design
(www.silverleafdesign.com)

Copyright © 2006 by Sigma Theta Tau International

Printed in the United States of America by V.G. Reed & Sons, Louisville, KY.

Sigma Theta Tau International
550 West North Street
Indianapolis, IN 46202

Visit our Web site at www.nursingknowledge.org/STTI/books for more information on our books and other knowledge services.

ISBN-10: 1-930538-44-8
ISBN-13: 978-1-930538-44-3

06 07 08 09 10 / 5 4 3 2 1

Library of Congress Cataloging-in-Publication Data

Briskin, Alan, 1954-
  Daily miracles : stories and practices of humanity and excellence in healthcare / by Alan Briskin and Jan Boller.
     p. ; cm.
  ISBN-13: 978-1-930538-44-3
  ISBN-10: 1-930538-44-8
  1. Nursing–Case studies. 2. Caring–Case studies. 3. Nurse and patient–Case studies.
I. Boller, Jan, 1947- II. Title.
  [DNLM: 1. Empathy. 2. Nursing Care–methods. 3. Nurse-Patient Relations. WY 86.5 B859d 2006]
RT41.B698 2006
610.73–dc22
                                                          2006033128

PREFACE

The creation of Daily Miracles was inspired by meetings with registered nurses who took time from their daily activities to reflect on what constitutes excellent care. The stories that came forward were spontaneous—only afterward did we encourage physically writing out the stories.

ACKNOWLEDGEMENTS

During the two years the nurses met, Gyana Bays, RN, joined us as co-steward of the dialogue. Her vision of caring and service to patients extends through every page of this book.

Gratitude to our thinking partners, Terry Glubka, RN, Joan Poole, RN, and Angela Anderson, RN, for their aid in imagining how best to organize the materials for optimal use.

Thanks and appreciation also go to Bev Gilmore and Janice Barnett, whose collective vision and support of this project made it possible. Special gratitude goes to Polly Gates, RN, for helping us, early on, to embark on this journey.

Acknowledgements and appreciation also go to Jane O'Brien, Sheryl Erickson of the Collective Wisdom Initiative, and Chérie Hafford of Silverleaf Design, for their partnership and craft with the book's design.

Appreciation goes to Ramón Lavandero, RN, MA, MSN, FAAN, director of development and strategic alliances, American Association of Critical-

Care nurses for making the introduction with the publishing team at Sigma Theta Tau International.

We are incredibly grateful to the leaders of Sutter Solano Medical Center for bringing this vision into the world.

We gratefully acknowledge the Fetzer Institute for its pioneering work on relationship-centered care.

Finally we offer our profound appreciation to the following individuals for their courage and contribution in sharing their stories for this book:

Nora Abena, RN	Gregory Coe, MD	Sharon Marks, RN
Myrna Aquino, RN	Judy Domenici, RN	Candis McCue, RN
Irene Arcibal, RN	Diane Garrison, RN	Diana Moises, RN
Pam Bentz, RN;	Nancy Hiteshew, RN	Chris Ramos, RN
Tom Bradley, RN	Socorro Layson, RN	Shauna Sarlatte, RN
Gina Cacuyog, RN	Divina Lumalu, RN	Jalynne Sousa, RN
Lily Cayabyab, RN	Celeste Madayag, RN	Susan Waters, MD

ABOUT THE AUTHORS

Alan Briskin
Photo by Sandy Simon

Alan Briskin, PhD, is author of the award-winning book *The Stirring of Soul in the Workplace* and co-founder of the Collective Wisdom Initiative (www.collectivewisdominitiative.org). In collaboration with Jan Boller and Gyana Bays, he designed and facilitated the two-year dialogue with nurses that led to this book. Alan is also a founding member of the Relationship-Centered Care Network, an innovative health care initiative seeking to promote the primacy of relationships to health and healing. Alan's Web site is www.alanbriskin.com

Jan Boller and her niece Sammy
Photo by Erica Thompson,
www.imagesforalifetime.com

Jan Boller, RN, PhD, has extensive experience as a clinical nurse educator, critical care nurse specialist, and scholar. She has held organizational leadership positions in the areas of clinical effectiveness and education, quality, case management, and clinical outcomes management. Jan's academic scholarship work has focused on the development of clinical nursing expertise. She is a health care systems consultant with AWR_Associates in Benicia, CA, and adjunct assistant professor at Samuel Merritt College in Oakland, CA. Jan's Web site is www.awrassociates.com.

TABLE OF CONTENTS

Introduction

n January of 2002, a group of nurse leaders came together at a community hospital in northern California with a shared desire for bringing compassion and excellence to the forefront of patient care. Charge nurses, staff nurses, supervisors, advanced practice nurses, and managers began with a common question: How does caring and compassion show up in the demanding and often chaotic experience of day-to-day practice?

There was no preconceived agenda or action plan, other than to share authentic experiences through dialogue, stories, personal insights, and group exploration. As these leaders began this journey, they knew that "the answers were in the room," but they had no idea where their dialogue would take them, or how the answers would present themselves. In all, this group met 23 times over two years. It was a time to pause in the rush of to-do's and be witnesses to their accomplishments and challenges. It was a time for renewal and support, seeing how the power to make a difference in their patients' lives also brought greater significance to their own. And it was an affirmation that when people are ill, they need a team to care for them, as do caregivers need to be part of a group that cares together.

This book brings to bear some of the beginning lessons learned in the form of stories and guiding principles. It illustrates tools that are fundamental to healing the human spirit. The stories, guiding principles, and tools together form the basis of a curriculum, keys to unlocking both clinical excellence and patient satisfaction.

What is Excellent Care?

WHAT IS EXCELLENT CARE?

Gregory M. Coe, MD

What we do in health care is unbelievably complex. When you examine the processes carefully and begin to identify all the components that need to work together, it is amazing. Those who work in the field are highly trained and extensively educated. The vast bulk of that training and education is focused on the technical and scientific aspects of what we do. Once you are well-learned in the field, the technical stuff becomes fairly easy, almost routine at times.

The real challenge comes when you put all of the science and technology into use with real people involved.

Patients come to us when they are vulnerable. They are frightened. They are in pain. They are overwhelmed. Their families and loved ones share those feelings. They all bring their dysfunctions and biases with them. They cannot be expected to be on their best behaviors.

Our world, the world of health care, is mostly foreign and frightening to them. Having to be in the hospital takes away their power, their control. They fear losing their dignity. They look to us for help.

To be just the scientist or the technologist is mediocre. To really help our patients, we must provide more. This means going beyond what is expected or assumed that we can do and doing what is unexpected. It is not enough to just cure the infection or bandage the wound. We must care for the patient.

We must care for them as whole persons. We must provide care for who they are, not merely for the affliction from which they suffer. We can come to understand and care about who they are. We can touch and connect with them. We can protect, maintain, and if necessary, restore their dignity. This is excellent care.

HELLO PROFESSOR

Irene Arcibal, RN

I was taking care of Mr. M. in the critical care unit (CCU). Mr.
M. was intubated and unable to wean. Every night I took
care of him. He could not respond or even follow simple
commands. If I was lucky, he opened his eyes when I called
his name, but still he did not follow any commands. I had the
feeling that he had given up.

One night, after my assessment, I saw a black book on top
of his night table. I thought it was a Bible, but it did not say
so on the cover. Out of curiosity, I picked it up and took it
to the desk. As I opened the book, I realized that it was a

psychology book. To my surprise, the book was written by my patient! "Wow! My patient is a writer," I thought.

I scanned through the pages until the last page, where it describes the author. Discovery, discovery—a great revelation indeed!

Mr. M. was a UCLA graduate with a master's degree and had taught in Japan for four years. Afterward, he had been a professor at UCLA for several years. I couldn't believe I was taking care of a professor.

I went into my patient's room and softly said, "Hello professor!" He opened his eyes, grabbed my hands, and then tears started coming out of his eyes. He smiled at me and squeezed my hands.

I believe that at that moment, I gave back to my patient his individuality and possibly his whole life.

ROOM 306 B

Chris Ramos, RN

Monday morning. I had not worked the weekend as had many of my co-workers. The shift began in the report room as the tape played information about each patient. The report of one patient played something like this: "Patient angry and critical of staff. Always coming to nurses' station demanding something, yet doesn't want to comply with treatment." As I listened to this, I heard a deep sigh from the other nurses. I thought they had probably had a tough weekend and were not up to dealing with a complicated patient today.

I volunteered to trade one of my patients for this patient if the charge nurse agreed.

I went from room to room greeting and assessing my patients. Finally, I came to 306 B and entered the room. Before I could introduce myself, 306 B was telling me how bad the night shift had been to her, and the PM shift before them was just as bad. She said she could not get anyone to listen or help her.

I stood there and let her tell me every negative thing she could come up with. When she stopped, I said "hello" and told her my name and that I would be her nurse today. I straightened up around her bed and bedside table as I talked to her about her pain, breathing, and so on. I asked her if she would mind sitting on the side of the bed so I could listen to her lungs.

I could feel how tight she was holding herself. I asked her if it would be all right with her if I rubbed her back. She agreed. I got some lotion and began to massage her back. As I did this, she began to tell me about her mother. She said the last one to massage her back had been her mom, who had died within the last year.

As she spoke, she cried, and as she cried she began to relax. She continued to tell me about her mom and the special things she had wanted to remember about her. I spent about 20 or 30 minutes rubbing her back. When I finished, she was in an entirely different state of mind. She said she felt so much better. I left the room. Sometime later, one of the other nurses said 306 B had gone to the nurses' station to apologize for being cranky and disagreeable.

Later, her doctor asked, "What happened to 306 B? She says she's ready to go home."

I learned an important lesson that day from 306 B. I learned that sometimes a bit of simple nurturing can go a long way. Listening can sometimes be the best medicine you can give someone. Later that day, I found out that 306 B's mother had died in this hospital and on this same floor. It made sense to me that she was anxious and demanding without having the skills to explain why.

STOPPING THE DOMINOS

Pam Bentz, RN

ursing. The job can be like dominos. You know about dominos—when you stand them up on end and just tap the first one, one by one they fall down. But if one domino is out of place, they stop falling.

It was late Friday afternoon, and it had been a busy day in the postanesthesia care unit. I was taking care of three post-operative patients. All three were waiting for beds in the med/surg unit. They were ready for transfer, but there were no beds available. Each patient had a spinal anesthetic, and the physicians' orders were for all to have PCA pumps for pain control (PCA pumps regulate continuous narcotic infusions). However, we had only one pump available. Although no one was experiencing any pain at the moment, they all wanted to get to a comfortable bed. I was getting frustrated. Nothing was going right.

I didn't like the fact that one of the patients noticed how stressed I was. He said to me, "Things aren't going well for you, are they?" And I had to admit to him, "No, they aren't." I pride myself on usually keeping my cool and not letting my patients notice if something isn't going well. But now I had let down my guard and let him see me get stressed about the situation. His comment made me step back, take a deep breath, and realize I could be that one domino that could stop the madness.

I got on the phone and explained to the doctor that we could order two rental PCAs, but they wouldn't be here until Monday. I knew these patients would be needing pain medication soon. I got pain medication orders, served the three patients juice and crackers, gave them their pain meds, apologized for getting caught up in things, and reassured them they would have beds soon.

Routinely, we call patients after they go home to see how they're doing. When I called the man who had noticed my stress, he was very complimentary about his care and specifically about the great job I had done.

I guess it was OK for us to share that "human moment" together. Even though I had temporarily lost my cool, with his help, I was able to "stop the dominos."

You, the nurse, can be that domino. You can stop the stressful, frustrating situations. So, step back, count to 10, and stop the dominos from falling. You can break the cycle.

"I THINK I KNOW YOU"

Nancy Hiteshew, RN

A patient with cancer was in triage, puking into the big bucket and yelling for blankets. "I'm cold," she said with anger and disgust. Her hair had fallen out from the chemotherapy treatments, and her face was swollen. When I handed her the blanket, she barked, "What are you looking at?"

"I'm looking into your eyes," I told her. "I think I know you. I'm trying to picture you with your hair." Her face softened and she started crying. "Before chemotherapy," she told me, "I had beautiful hair."

Something shifted in that moment between us. It was OK. She didn't seem angry any longer.

Often we are confronted with the fear, anger, and despair of our patients, but there are moments when our own presence of mind and caring intent can change that.

SAVING GRACE

Nancy Hiteshew, RN

On a day so horrible and bad, we all just worked hard and no one complained. Dr. C. called the next day and thanked us all.

He wanted us to know how much he appreciated us. What a difference it makes in one's day.

PLAYING THE PONIES

Gina Cacuyog, RN

r. G. appeared anxious and frightened, knowing he was to undergo cardioversion (shock to the heart with electrical impulses). He demanded to see his doctor, who was unavailable.

I had planned to do nothing else but drop off the machine, which, when he saw it, only frightened him further. He asked me who I was and said he thought he knew me. I asked if he had been a patient in the critical care unit.

Suddenly we connected. We have the same hobby, at least one of mine–playing the ponies. Soon we were talking and then he was laughing. Now, more relaxed, he was treated successfully.

Somehow our connection–just two people who played the ponies–reassured him. How unexpected. How satisfying.

LOST IN THE HOSPITAL

Tom Bradley, RN

It was a typical night in the ER. This particular patient was a man in his mid 60s who had just had a heart attack. He also happened to live four houses down the street from me. He needed cardiac catheterization and transportation to a facility in Oakland. Time being of the essence and the ambulance service delayed in finding a critical care nurse, I opted to ride along with the patient on the way to the medical center.

The patient was stable but still apprehensive and nervous about his condition. The ride was uneventful, and the paramedic crew I was traveling with seemed to know the area, so I was blindly following. We arrived just before 5 AM. There were several detours in the hallways as the hospital was under construction. The hallways were empty and the medics were acting confused. They really did not know their way around, and we were lost in the hospital.

Nurses were nowhere to be found, and we were going from floor to floor looking for the "cath lab." After what seemed like a very long time and multiple elevator rides, the patient looked up at me from the gurney and said, "You really don't know where you are going, do you?"

Trying not to worry him, I just smiled and said, "No I don't, but there are people here who will show us." At this point he laughed and the tension eased. We found the cath lab, with the help of several employees, and his recovery was successful.

I did not see him for almost two years after that night. I stopped by his house one day while out walking with my wife. He told me his life had changed from that day on. He had retired immediately from his engineering job. He devoted his life to his wife, his family, and his religion. They bought a motor home and traveled together. He said he walked two miles a day and had changed his whole lifestyle. He even made his two sons (in their 40s) have diagnostic studies done. Both of them had significant coronary disease and both were treated prior to having major problems. His wife told me that he constantly preaches to his sons about stress and living a good life.

This is my story about the patient who said, "You don't know where you are going, do you?"

Often we don't get the feedback on the good that we do and how illness can turn a person's life in a positive direction—even when our own sense of direction may be challenged.

Guiding Principles

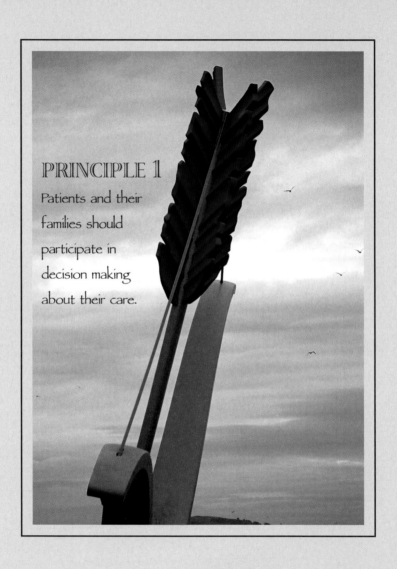

PRINCIPLE 1

Patients and their
families should
participate in
decision making
about their care.

PRINCIPLE 2

Healing has many dimensions.

PRINCIPLE 3

Through grace, we
add a
measure of healing
by sharing
a human
connection
with
the patient
as a
person.

A comfortable
relationship is in itself
a
reassuring action.

PRINCIPLE 4

Patients and their families should receive support and compassion to ease life/death transitions.

More Daily Miracles
Stories of Caring and Excellence

LISTENING TO METAPHORS

Jan Boller, RN

In health care, death becomes part of our speech as both literal reality and as metaphor—a symbol often of fear and everything we should be against. The fear of death is frequently viewed as motivating to patients, but often its effect isn't.

A wonderful example was given by Marion who was told by a physician that if she didn't stop smoking she would die of lung cancer. Later, she had a conversation with a respiratory therapist, and he asked her if she smoked.

She said "Yes, and I know you're going to tell me to stop."

He said, "No, I'm not."

Then he asked her "How much do you spend every day to smoke?"

She replied "$4.32."

He started calculating in his head and said, "Do you know what that amounts to in a year?"

"No," replied Marion.

He said, "Enough to take a luxury cruise in the Caribbean."

Guess which advice stimulated her to stop smoking?

With the first, all she could think about was that she was going to die. With the second, she thought about possibilities and living.

Marion referred to the respiratory therapist as one of the two compassionate people she had encountered in her hospitalization for asthma and pneumonia (the other was an environmental service person who cleaned her room).

But bundled into that compassion was a conversation that convinced her to stop smoking. He gave her a metaphor, that of a Caribbean cruise, linked to living well rather than to suffering and death.

What if we tried using more metaphors of living in all our conversations?

THE BEST SEAT IN THE HOUSE

Jan Boller, RN

I t was 3 July, the day before the U.S. national Independence Day holiday, and there was an elderly woman in the transitional care unit (TCU) who was scheduled to be discharged that day. As the staff and her family were making preparations for her to leave, she kept coming up with all kinds of aches and pains, coughing, and other problems. She did not want to go, and the staff and her family kept telling her that she did not need to stay here and that another patient needed her room.

She kept persisting so the staff called in Dr. W. In conversation, Dr. W. discovered she wanted to stay to see the fireworks at Marine World the following evening.

Dr. W. pulled out her prescription pad. She wrote: "Mrs. P. and her family are to be the guests of Dr. W. on the 4th Floor to view the fireworks on July 4th."

The security guards, (who were watching the hospital parking lot to discourage non hospital visitors) reported that the patient and her family returned the next evening to watch the fireworks. They handed the prescription to the security guard and were personally escorted to the "best seat in the house."

What a difference we can make when we respond to the ache of the heart.

KIND WORDS

Irene Arcibal, RN

I had taken care of her since she was placed on a respirator. When the respirator finally came off, I told her how happy I was to hear her voice.

Later, in the middle of my shift, while I was turning her, she said, "Thank you for your help. You are a beautiful person."

FINAL REQUEST

Judy Domenici, RN, and Irene Arcibal, RN

M r. H. was dying in the critical care unit (CCU). His wife had broken her hip, and she was in the med/surg unit on the 3rd floor. We requested she be brought down to the CCU.

Together, they just held each other's hands. No one disturbed them ... such a peaceful, overwhelming, and heartwarming moment.

Philosophy of Care

HOLISTIC PHILOSOPHY

The whole person and his or her relationships, including family, loved ones, and care-givers, is our focus: mind–body–spirit.

We Can:

- Speak without medical jargon.

- Speak respectfully about the progression of illness.

- Aid patients and families to cope and to find peace, comfort, and higher meaning.

- Develop our capacity as caregivers to address the spiritual concerns of our patients and families.

- Speak with people who can find solutions.

GUIDING QUESTIONS

- How can we empower our patients to maintain and regain control over their wellbeing and recuperation?

- How can we offer our patients a variety of ways to be comfortable, to be calmed, to relax, and to be in a better frame of mind?

- How can we create comfort and connection through relationships?

- How can we make it possible for the patient to pass with dignity, grace, and love?

CREATING CARE PARTNERSHIPS

- Bring the patient and family into the center of care.

- Follow the rhythm of the patient and family to know what is most important and when.

- Stimulate the patient's interests regarding the disease process and the options for healing and health.

- Help the patients find their role in the healing process.

- Create an environment where patients feel cared for by how we demonstrate curiosity about their physical, emotional, and spiritual state.

OUR COMMITMENT TO EXCELLENCE

- To provide professional caregivers who believe that a person's participation in his or her own care strongly influences the outcome of healing practices.

- To provide professional caregivers who are able to break down barriers to learning, through communication and family involvement.

- To provide opportunities to reflect and to acknowledge illness as a part of life with the potential to alter a person's life for the better.

- To educate people about the power of self-care and to offer options and choices for facilitating healing and health.

END-OF-LIFE TRANSITIONS

- At orientation—sharing the expectation that the natural process of death is acknowledged, holding the same level of importance as the curative plan of care.

- At the bedside—creating a place for privacy in which family members can say good-bye.

- In hiring—recruiting and training staff who have an understanding and respect for the dying process.

- In staff development—ongoing education and support for those who provide care at the end of life.

- Day-to-day—bringing in staff that may best be able to "resonate" with the patient and family.

- In larger community—engage staff members and the community in a program so that "No One Dies Alone."

PRACTICES THAT WORK

We will greet you by your name ("Hello, Mr. ___").

When we meet you, we will introduce ourselves, our role, and what we will be doing for you.

Whenever possible, we will sit by your bedside as we have our conversations.

We will ask you about your beliefs about your illness, what your expectations are about your care, and what you feel helps you recover and heal.

We will ask you what is important for you right now (your main concern that we might be able to help you with.)

We will also notice what may be signs of concern and ask, e.g. "You seem tense." "Are you having pain right now?"

As we care for you, we will let you know what we are doing and why.

When you leave the hospital, we will prepare you for what to expect and how to care for yourself.

We will notice what makes you special, such as photos, the warmth of your smile, and your interests.

As we leave your room, we will ask you, "Is there anything else that I can do for you right now?"

If we say we will do something, we will let you know when we think you can expect to get an answer or resolution. (We will be realistic.)

If we say we will do something, we will follow up later to let you know it was done and check to see if it was resolved to your satisfaction.

We will walk out of the room backwards. That is, as we leave the room, we will check to see if you are comfortable and keep facing you as long as we talk with you. At the same time, we will notice anything about your room environment that may not be right—clutter, room temperature, noise, availability of the call light, phone, TV control, bedside table, etc.

Our attention, actions, and words will show that we care.

RECENTLY PUBLISHED BOOKS
FROM THE HONOR SOCIETY OF NURSING

Pivotal Moments in Nursing: Leaders Who Changed the Path of a Profession, Volume I (2004) and Volume II (2006), by Beth P. Houser and Kathy N. Player.

When Parents Say No: Religious and Cultural Influences on Pediatric Healthcare Treatment, by Luanne Linnard-Palmer (2006).

Healthy Places, Healthy People: A Handbook for Culturally Competent Community Nursing Practice, by Melanie C. Dreher, Dolores J. Shapiro, and Micheline Asselin (2006).

The beautiful art book, The HeART of Nursing: Expressions of Creative Art in Nursing, Second Edition, edited by M. Cecilia Wendler (2005).

Reflecting on 30 Years of Nursing Leadership: 1975-2005, by Sr. Rosemary Donley (2005).

The Making a Difference series of books, including A Daybook for Nurses (2004), Making a Difference: Stories from the Point of Care, Volume I and Volume II, by Sharon Hudacek (2004/2005).

The beautiful full-color book, Ordinary People, Extraordinary Lives: The Stories of Nurses, edited by Carolyn Hope Smeltzer and Frances R. Vlasses (2003).